Inspirational Quotes
and
Thoughts

Inspirational Quotes and Thoughts

Compiled by
G C Beri

V&SPUBLISHERS

Published by:

$\mathcal{V}$&S PUBLISHERS

F-2/16, Ansari Road, Daryaganj, New Delhi-110002
011-23240026, 011-23240027 • *Fax:* 011-23240028
Email: info@vspublishers.com • *Website:* www.vspublishers.com

Regional Offi ce : Hyderabad
5-1-707/1, Brij Bhawan (Beside Central Bank of India Lane)
Bank Street, Koti, Hyderabad - 500 095
040-24737290
E-mail: vspublishershyd@gmail.com

Branch Offi ce : Mumbai
Flat No. Ground Floor, Sonmegh Building
No. 51, Karel Wadi, Thakurdwar, Mumbai - 400 002
022-22098268
E-mail: vspublishersmum@gmail.com

Follow us on:

For any assistance sms **VSPUB** to **56161**

All books available at **www.vspublishers.com**

© **Copyright: Author**
ISBN 978-81-920796-3-9
Edition 2014

Printed at : Param Offseters, Okhla, New Delhi-110020

Contents

Preface

Life is a series of ups and downs. As long as things are in our favour fulfilling our expectations, we are happy and wish that this happiness should never end. But we all know that this seldom happens. While this is true, it is also a fact that misfortune can occur at any time in life. It could be anything - failure in examination, rejection in a job interview, loss in business, illness, stressful family life or even divorce. Amidst such problems, our immediate reaction is of confusion, depression, or even helplessness. While in distress the presence of timely advice can prove to be very helpful. The book is an attempt in this direction.

It gives me great pleasure in presenting this book, a comprehensive compilation of words of wisdom. It has been an enlightening and fulfilling effort for me to put together a large number of quotes drawn from varied sources. Reading has been a passion for me since my student days. My favourites include topics like the art of living, personality development, yoga and spirituality. Whenever I'd come across a passage or quote that was appealing, I'd note it down. The fascination resulted in a huge collection of quotes; something I deemed appropriate to publish in the form of a book. There are close to 460 quotes, classified under nineteen groups on the basis of their content; with the exception of the last one that lies under the group Miscellaneous.

I sincerely hope that amidst difficulties and setbacks, a glance through the book, can be illuminating and inspiring, enabling the reader to come out of depression and sadness and develop a positive attitude which is so important for success and happiness in life.

G C Beri

BOOKS AND READING HABIT

Reading maketh a full man; conference a ready man; and writing an exact man.

– Francis Bacon

A home without books is a body without soul.

– Marcus Tullius

To learn to read is to light a fire; every syllable that is spelled out is a spark.

– Victor Hugo

To read without reflecting is like eating without digesting.

– Edmund Burke

What is wonderful about great literature is that it transforms the man who reads it towards the condition of the man who wrote.

– E.M. Forster

If I read a book and it makes my body so cold no fire can ever warm me, I know its poetry.

– Emily Dickinson

If one cannot enjoy reading a book over and over again; there is no use in reading it at all.

– Oscar Wilde

Some books are to be tasted, others to be swallowed, and some few to be chewed and digested.

– Francis Bacon

Every man who knows how to read has it in his power to magnify himself, to multiply the ways in which he exists, to make his life full, significant and interesting.

– Aldous Huxley

A good book is the best of friends, the same today and tomorrow.

– Martin Tupper

Don't just say you have read books. Show that through them you have learned to think better, to be a more discriminating and reflected person. Books are the training weights of the mind. They are very helpful, but it would be a bad mistake to suppose that one has made progress simply by having internalized their contents.

– Epictetus

Read, not to contradict and confute; not to believe and take for granted, not to find talk and discourse, but to weigh and consider.

– Francis Bacon

The best books elevate us into a region of disinterested thought, where personal objects fade into insignificance, and the troubles and anxieties of the world are almost forgotten.

– Lord Avebury

Reading good books can be of help in the early mental stage - they prepare the mind, put it in the right atmosphere, can even, if one is very sensitive, bring some glimpses of realization on the mental plane. Afterwards the utility diminishes - you have to find every knowledge and experience in yourself.

– Sri Aurobindo

Reading contributes significantly to the success and development of an individual and it is recommended for people of all demographics. Many recent surveys done across the world have found that reading habits have diminished, especially in managers who should be reading extensively.

– Nitya Sai Souniya

The more that you read, the more things you will know. The more that you learn, the more places you'll go.

– Dr. Seuss

Study as if you were to live for ever, live as if you were to die tomorrow.

– Mahatma Gandhi

Being open to, and actively seeking new knowledge is a lesson that must be quickly learned if success and happiness are your goal.

– Greg Vance

Books are the quietest and most constant of friends; they are the most accessible and wisest of counsellors and then most patient of teachers.

– Charles W. Eliot

To get the greatest amount not merely of benefit but even of enjoyment from books, we must read for improvement, rather than for amusement.

– Lord Avebury

A man should be known by the books he reads and collects. There is a common trait among book lovers. They are always eager and even anxious to get more and more books, to the extent of getting irritated if they do not get the desired ones and angry if some from the collection are lost or misplaced.

– Govind Talwalkar

CHANGE

Change is a gift from God, a doorway to the next spiritual level, and we are a creative force in our own lives. To no longer be the victim of change is to master change. This mastery allows you to see the hand of God at work in your life and create a future that reflects confidence, a divine plan and a higher purpose.

– Mary Carroll Moore

Change is not only inevitable; it is constant and unvarying law. Without it, everything would remain for ever as it is, and there could be neither growth nor progress.

– James Allen

Every change in life offers new experiences, and each new experience is an opportunity of further development. This is why, if we refuse to go forward voluntarily, life tumbles us out of our comfortable little niche and throws us into the maelstrom -that we may become wiser, more capable men and women.

– S. Harrison

There is no doubt that the timid soul shrinks from making a radical change in life, from stepping forth into the unknown; but to compel oneself to do this is to take out the finest possible insurance for the happiness of the years to come. To stay in the same rut year after year means that life passes us by. We realize when it is too late that we have never truly lived -for we have shirked life.

– S. Hal-rison

To resist change is to work against the flow of life rather than surrender to and trust it.

– Susan Taylor

We do not succeed in changing things according to our desire, but gradually our desire changes.

– Marcel Proust

A turning point is life's way of giving you a chance to move ahead spiritually, though you must reach for the gift yourself.

– Harold Klemp

We begin the process of transforming all those things we usually consider stumbling blocks into the stepping stones they really are.

– Rick Fields

Change is not made without inconvenience, even from worse to better.

– Samuel Johnson

If we want to live fully, beyond the life we have today, we must take risks, stretch, ourselves, move past what we are now.

– Marsha Sinetar

Everything teaches transition, transference, metamorphosis: therein is human power. We dive and reappear in new places.

– Ralph Waldo Emerson

If there is any law which governs human existence it is the law of change. We forget it at our peril. Most ancient societies forgot it and suffered.

– Paul Brunton

While we cannot change the past, with the wisdom of Spirit we can change what it remains to us and to our future.

– Susan Tylor

EDUCATION

Education is not just going to school for a few years and learning a thing or two fairly well, and a few bits and pieces of others -that is, it is not what it usually becomes in practice or is taken to be. It is a leading forward, a leading out, which is the root meaning of the word.

– Jesse Roarke

True education will nurture noble character rather than egoistic calculation, foster sharp intelligence rather than routine memory, train the student to the kind of technical work he or she likes to do and can do, and teach things of lasting value rather than force useless ones into the mind.

– Paul Brunton

Student-life should refine and develop the best qualities of human nature, enlighten the mind of the student, equip him to meet the challenges of life, and infuse in him the understanding of the ultimate reality behind all phenomena.

– Swami Sivananda

To my mind, education is the spirit of enquiry, the ability to keep one's mind and heart open to beauty and goodness, indeed all that surrounds us, to be able to think and judge for oneself. Education should inculcate a life long habit of learning.

And today, this is all the more necessary because the corpus of knowledge is increasing at a tremendous pace, often making what one has learnt obsolete.

– Indira Gandhi

I am persuaded that the best education in the world is that which we insensibly acquire form conversation with our intellectual superiors.

– Bulwer

We learn not at school, but in life.

– Seneca

There is only one corner of the Universe you can be certain of improving and that is your own self.

– Aldous Leonard Huxley

Children should be taught to look for beauty everywhere, to read the great poem of creation in the great panorama of Nature.

– Orison Swett Marden

Of what use is an education if it does not teach the young how to use their minds so as to promote their own welfare, instead of their own harm? All ought to be made aware of the value and need of emotional and thought control, of discriminating between destructive or negative thoughts and constructive or positive ones.

– Paul Brunton

The illiterates of the 21st century will not be those who cannot read and write, but those who cannot learn, unlearn, and relearn.

– Alvin Toffler

I have never in my life learned anything from any man who agreed with me.

– Dudley Field Malone

A teacher affects eternity, he can never tell where his influence stops.

-Henry Brooks Adams

Education is the most powerful weapon which you can use to change the world.

– Nelson Mandela

Human nature is fundamentally good and the spread of enlightenment will abolish all wrong. Vice is only a miss, an error. We can learn to become good. Virtue is teachable.

– Dr. S. Radhakrishnan

Acquire new knowledge while thinking over old, and you may become a teacher of others.

– Confucius

A liberally educated person meets new ideas with curiosity and fascination. An illiberally educated person meets new ideas with fear.

– James B. Stockdale

A school is a place where one learns about the totality, the wholeness of life. Academic excellence is absolutely necessary, but a school includes much more than that. It is a place where both the teacher and the student explore, not only the outer world, the world of knowledge, but also their own thinking, their own behaviour.

– J. Krishnamurti

We want that education by which character is formed, strength of mind is increased, the intellect is expanded, and by which one can stand on one's own feet.

– Swami Vevekananda

Education's purpose is to replace an empty mind with an open one.

– Malcolm Forbes

The main goal of education is to teach people to think.

– Lord Cromer

The first duty of a university is to teach wisdom, not trade, character, not technicalities.

– Winston Churchill

In school you're taught a lesson and then given a test. In life, you're given a test that teaches you a lesson.

– Tom Bodtt

An open mind is the beginning of self-discovery and growth. We can't learn anything new until we can admit that we don't already know everything.

– Erwin G. Hall

Being ignorant is not so much a shame as being unwilling to learn to do things the right way.

– Benjamin Franklin

Education develops the features of politeness, cordiality, forbearance, perseverance and discipline etc. To face the various challenges that life puts forward, knowledge is imperative and we should strive towards earning this wealth all the time.

– Gangadhar Pandey

Education at its best is a process of liberation from prejudice which frees the human heart from its violent passions. It is through education that young people can be delivered from powerlessness, from the burden of mistrust directed against themselves. And those who have learned to trust in themselves are then naturally able to believe in the latent capacities of others.

– Dr. Daisaku Ikeda

No system of Education will ever be worth what it costs until it trains the wants of our children. How to gratify the wants that are legitimate? How to restrain the wants that are unsocial? If teachers cannot do this, of what moral use is it to do anything else?

– Herbert Casson

A student gets forms, rules, and guidebooks in college, but he must get power from actual contact with the acting, living world.

– Orison Swett Marden

The great man was not great when he started his career. Neither was he wise. But he made himself great and wise by learning-learning-learning.

– Herbert Casson

Knowledge is a child with its achievements, for it has found out something, it runs about the streets whooping and shouting; Wisdom conceals her for a long time in a thoughtful and mighty silence.

– Sri Aurobindo

Surely, education has no meaning unless it helps you to understand the vast expanse of life with all to subtleties, with its extraordinary beauty, its sorrows and joys. You may earn degrees; you may have a series of letters after your name and land a very good job, but then what? What is the point of if in the process your mind becomes full, weary, stupid?

– J. Krishnamurti

Who dares to teach must never cease to learn.

– John Cotton Dana

Acquire new knowledge while thinking over old, and you may become a teacher of others.

– Confucius

I like learning, Learning is beautiful.

– Natalie Portman

Education is discipline for the adventure of life.

– A. North Whitehead

FAILURE

If you are willing to accept failure and learn from it, if you are willing to consider failure as a blessing in disguise and bounce back, you have got the potential of harnessing one of the most powerful success forces.

– Joseph Sugarman

Don't be afraid to fail. Don't waste energy trying to cover up failure. Learn from failures and go on to the next challenge. It is OK to fail. If you are not failing you are not growing.

– H. Stanley Judd

I would rather fail in a cause that will ultimately succeed than succeed in a cause that would ultimately fail.

– Woodrow Wilson

There are some defeats more triumphant than victories.

– Michel de Montaigne

Develop success from failures. Discouragement and failure are two of the surest stepping stones to success.

– Dale Carnagie

A life spent in making mistakes is not only more honourable but more useful than a life spent doing nothing.

– George Bernard Shaw

We begin the process of transforming all those things we usually consider stumbling blocks into the stepping stones they really are.

– Rick Fields

The man who makes no mistakes does not usually make anything.

– William Connor Magee

It is when you accept failure that you are a failure. Not he who is handicapped by illness, nor he who is constantly trying in spite of repeated setbacks, but he who is physically and mentally lazy is the real failure. The person, who refuses to think, or reason, or discriminate, or use his will or creative energy, is already dead.

– Yogananda

No one can say that he has never tasted failure in life. Life means ups and downs; sometimes you are up and sometimes you are down, it is never the same. The important lesson to remember is that you should keep struggling all the time, no matter what the results are. You should continue with your struggle even when there is a success, for it is possible to improve upon the success you have so far achieved.

– Swami Lokeswarananda

FAITH

Faith is one of the forces by which men live and the total absence of it means collapse.

– William James

Faith in oneself and faith in God - these are the key to success and achievement.

– Swami Jagadatmananda

The greatest secret for eliminating the infirmity complex, which is another term for deep and profound self - doubt, is to fill your mind to overflowing faith. Develop a tremendous faith in God and that will give you a humble yet soundly realistic faith in yourself.

– Norman Vincent Peale

Faith is what gives us the power to keep going long after we know that we have been defeated. Faith is what gives us the strength to fight beyond our strength.

– M.V. Kamath

The one who has faith in himself will never doubt other things, he will build his resolve on his ideal and fling himself resolutely after it.

– Julie Seton

Faith is one of the potent factors of humanity and of all religions.

-Swarmi Vivekananda

Have faith that you are all born to do great things. Let not the barks of puppies frighten you - no, not even the thunderbolts of heaven - but stand up and work.

– Swami Vivekanand

Faith is the sustaining power in every enterprise of any magnitude; without it no great achievement would ever be possible.

– S. Harrison

Faith is an essential instrument to overcome the difficulties in pursuing right and religious path. Development of faith is of paramount importance. But one should be very cautious about rational faith and blind faith. The former is cause of progress and prosperity of all sorts, while latter leads to hell.

-Shri Ram Sharma Acharya

All the great inventions of mankind have materialized as the result of immense, unshakable faith on the part of the inventor. Only such all - conquering faith could have enabled man to persevere in the face of repeated failure and disheartening opposition.

– S. Harrison

Nothing in this world was ever accomplished without living faith.

– Mahatma Gandhi

Have enough faith in your divine heritage, take it into your common everyday life and thought, and in some way, to some people, you will become very significant and important.

– Paul Brunton

Faith can fight despair, and win, too. Look upon your difficulties not as stumbling blocks to trip you up, but as things waiting to be conquered.

– Paul Brunton

FATE

This duel experience of fate on the one hand, and freedom on the other, has given rise to the interminable controversy between the believers in fatalism and the upholders of free will.

– James Allen

My fate is in my own hands. If it is to be it is upto me to get on and do it. I am in control and life is a 'do-it-to-self process, not a 'being-done- to' process.

– Greg Vance

Everything that is happening to us is in accordance with the law of karma. What is happening to us today is only what we did in the past returning to us. Therefore, let us hold no grudge in our heart against anyone. Let us explain to ourselves that old accounts are being settled.

– Dada J.P. Vaswani

Destiny is not a matter of chance. It is a matter of choice. It is not a thing to be waited for, it is a thing to be achieved.

– W.J. Bryan

Man is architect of his own destiny. Fate or destiny is nothing more than the shadow of action and exertion ..... The key to success is neither with fate nor with the astrologers, palmists, pundits, purohits and temples etc.

– Shriram Sharma Acharya

Each one of us is the maker of his own fate.

– Swami Vivekananda

Fate moves in rhythms of gain or loss, in cycles of accumulation and deprivation. The force which brings us loving friends and hating enemies is one and the same.

– Paul Brunton

There is no such thing as accident or chance or fate or luck in life excepting the results of one's own previous actions which have all these appellations.

– Swami Omkarananda

It is man's ignorance, which makes him feel that he is weak, and that he is ever dependent on the invisible land of fate. This ignorance will lead him only to his degradation. To utilize the present is to conquer the fate.

– Swami Jagadatmanada

The unity between our character and our destiny is inseparable; the connection between our way of thinking and the course of events is unerring.

– Paul Brunton

The Indian explanation of fate is Karma. We ourselves are our own fate through our actions, but the fate created by us binds us; for what we have sown, we must reap in this life or another. Still we are creating our fate for the future even while undergoing old fate from the past in the present.

– Sri Aurobidno

FEAR

What do you have to fear? Whom do you have to fear? No one? Why? Because whoever has joined forces with God obtains three great privileges: omnipotence without power, intoxication without wine, and life without death....

– Francis of Assissi

No passion so effectively robs the mind of all its powers of acting and reasoning as fear.

– Edmund Burke

Nothing is so much to be feared as fear.

– Henry David Thoreau

We should not let our fears hold us back from pursuing our hopes.

– John F. Kennedy

The effect of fear on one's general health is depressive, since it constricts breathing and the circulation of blood: the action of the heart is restricted and breathing is shallow. The whole system in consequence becomes impoverished.

– S. Harrison

Fear is a sign of weakness. It is fear that is the great cause of misery in the world.

– Swami Vivekananda

I am not discouraged, because every wrong attempt discarded is another step forward.

– Thomas Edison

So long as you are dominated by fear you cannot enjoy perfect health......And fear has just as harmful an effect on one's efficiency as on one's health.

– S. Harrison

To fear disease, failure or trouble is to sow seeds in the subconscious field that will bring forth a harvest of diseased conditions, troubled thoughts, confused mental states and misdirected actions in body and mind.

– Christian D. Larson

I feel quite sure that nothing makes people age faster than fear.

– Deepak Chopra

The best way to overcome the habit of fear is to assure the mental attitude of courage, just as the best way to get rid of darkness is to let in the light.

– William Walker Atkinson

Fear stands as a gloomy sentinel and will not let the spirit pass into possession of its best. The strands of failure are made from the fibres of fear; wherever fear is active, failure is its neighbour.

– Julie Seton

HAPPINESS

Neither wealth nor rank will ensure happiness. Without love and charity and peace of mind you may be rich, great and powerful, but you cannot be happy.

– Lord Avebury

Happiness lies not in the mere possession of wealth. It lies in the joy of achievement, in the thrill of creative effort.

– Franklin D. Roosevelt

Work faithfully, and you will put yourself in possession of a glorious and enlarging happiness.

– Orison Swett Marden

It is no one's fault but our own if we are unhappy; it is no one's fault but our own if we are sick, poor, or full of lack. The whole scheme of existence makes for happiness and all life is full, complete, serene, only awaiting our own awakening to that fact.

– Julia Seton

Happiness depends to some extent upon external conditions, but chiefly upon mental attitudes. In order to be happy one should have good health, a well-balanced mind, a prosperous life, the right work, a thankful heart, and, above all, wisdom or knowledge of God.

– Yogananda

So long as you persist in selfishly seeking your own personal happiness, so long will happiness elude you, and you will be sowing the seeds of wretchedness. In so far as you succeed in losing yourself in the service of others, in that measure will happiness come to you, and you will reap a harvest of bliss.

– James Allen

When the mind is without fear and head is held high, when knowledge flows freely, where the world is not broken up in narrower cells, where words come out of depth of the heart, there bliss follows.

– Ravindra Nath Tagore

Real happiness is not in the senses but above the senses.

– Swami Vivekananda

The supreme happiness of life is the conviction that we are loved, - loved for ourselves, or rather, loved in spite of ourselves.

– Victor Hugo

It is neither wealth nor splendour, but tranquillity and occupation, which give happiness.

– Thomas Jefferson

You traverse the world in search of happiness which is within the reach of every man; a contended mind confers it all.

– Horace

It is a foolish idea to suppose that another person can cause us happiness or misery.

– Buddha

True bliss is a state where adversity and sorrow do not exist, an ever contented state - it is like a medicine which in the beginning appears bitter, but in truth, purifies from within.

– Mahatma Gandhi

Happiness is that inward state of perfect satisfaction which is joy and peace, and form which all desire is culminated.... The giving up of desire is the realisation of heaven, and all delights await the pilgrim there.

– James Allen

LIFE

One of the secrets of life is to make stepping stones out of stumbling blocks.

– James Penn

Life is a grindstone, whether it grinds you down or polishes you up depends on what you are made of.

– Jacod M. Brande

Your living is determined not so much by what life brings to you as by the attitude you bring to life; not so much by what happens to you as by the way your mind looks at what happens.

– John Homer Miller

Time is life. It is irreversible and irreplaceable. To waste your time is to waste your life, but to master your time is to master your life and make the most of it.

– Alan Lakein

Life is a series of problems. Do we want to moan about them or solve them?

– M. Scott Peek

The main purpose of life is to live rightly, think rightly and act rightly.

– Mahatma Gandhi

It seems strange that although we all love life so dearly, cling to it with such desperate tenacity, we should sell it so cheaply, should deliberately throw away so many precious years, by wrong living and bad thinking.

– Orison Swett Marden

I look at life from both sides now
From win and lose and still somehow
It's life's illusions I recall
I really don't know life at all.

– Joni Mitchell

We are taught to fly in the air like birds, and to swim in the water like fishes, but how to live on the earth we do not know.

– Dr. S. Radha Krishnan

There are two ways to live your life - one is as though nothing is miracle, the other is as though everything is miracle.

– Albert Einsten

One of the greatest adventures in living is getting to know yourself better. It is a tragedy that some individuals spend a lifetime going nowhere, bogged down in frustration, because they don't know anything about themselves or how to cope with problems, many created by environment.

– Dr. Maxwall Maltz

A life spent in making mistakes is not only more honourable but more useful than a life spent doing nothing.

– George Bernard Shaw

A life merely of pleasure, or chiefly of pleasure, is always a poor and worthless life, not worth the living; always unsatisfactory in its course, always miserable in its end.

– Theodore Parker

The man who has lived longest is not the man who counted most years, but he who has enjoyed life most.

– Rousseau

The quality of a person's life is in direct proportion to his commitment to excellence, regardless of his chosen field of endeavour.

-Victor Lonbaradt

Life is no brief candle for me. It is a sort of splendid torch which I have got hold for the moments, and I want to make it burn as brightly as possible before handing it on to future generations.

– George Bernard Shaw

Destiny is not a matter of chance. It is a matter of choices. It is not a thing to be waited for; it is a thing to be achieved.

– W.J. Bryan

Life is not the designed plan of a Divine artist. It is merely an accident in a mechanical universe, but we can make it, if we will, a happy or at least an interesting accident.

– Epicurus

Life is like a game of chess, in which there are a number of complex moves possible. The choice is open, but the move contains within itself all future moves. One is free to choose, but what follows is the result of one's choice. From the consequences of one's actions, there is never any escape.

– Shelly Smith

Life is a journey from impurity to purity, from hatred to cosmic love, from death to immortality, from imperfection to perfection, from slavery to freedom, from diversity to unity, from ignorance to eternal wisdom, from pain to eternal bliss, from weakness to infinite strength.

– Swami Sivananda

In three words I can sum up everything I have learned about life: it goes on.

– Robert Frost

Life is partly what we make it, and partly what it is made by the friends we choose.

-Tennessee Williams

Creating a successful life might be as simple as determining which are the most valuable, and seeing how many of those I can string together in a line.

– Pam Houston

Life has a practice of living you if you don't live it.

– Philip Larkin

Stand up, be bold, be strong. Take the whole responsibility on your shoulders and know that you are the creator of your own destiny. All the strength and succour you want is within yourself. Therefore make your own future.

-Swami Vivekananda

I know of no more encouraging fact than the unquestionable ability of man to elevate his life by conscious endeavour.

– Henry David Thoreau

I often think, it would be best not to attempt the solution of problem of life. Living is hard enough without complicating the process by thinking about it. The wisest thing, perhaps, is to take for granted, "the wearisome condition of humanity, born under one law to another bound" and to leave the matter at that without an attempt to reconcile the incompatibles.

– Aldous Huxley

I believe in facing life in an adventurous way going ahead with it without shouting or making noise.

– Jawaharlal Nehru

Make it a rule of life never to regret and never to look back. Regret is an appalling waste of energy. You cannot build on it, it is only good for wallowing on.

– Katherine Mansfield

The man who regards his life and that of his fellow creatures as meaningless is not merely unfortunate but almost disqualified for life.

– Albert Einstein

We are not only what we know of ourselves but an immense more which we do not know; and momentary personality is only a bubble on the ocean of our existence.

– Sri Aurobindo

Life is a series of lessons. Some are diligent in learning them, and they become pure, wise, and altogether happy. Others are negligent, and do not apply themselves. They remain impure, foolish, and unhappy.

– James Allen

The good news is that the best season of your life can be ahead of you no matter what your age or circumstances-if you choose to make it so-because 90 percent of your potential is not only untapped, but also undiscovered. That's not just news, it's incredible news!

– Tim Hamsel

To be what we are, and to become what we are capable of becoming, is the only end of life.

– Robert Louis Stevenson

God asks no man whether he will accept life. That is not the choice. You must take it. The only choice is how.

– Henry Ward Beecher

One cannot participate in this mysterious act of living with any hope of satisfaction unless one understands a few simple rules.

– Og Mandino

The overvaluation of money, status, and competition poisons our personal relations. The flourishing life cannot be achieved until we moderate our desires and see how superficial and fleeting they are.

– Epictetus

All human beings seek the happy life, but many confuse the means - for example, wealth and status - with that life itself. This misguided focus on the means to a good life makes people get further from the happy life. The really worthwhile things are the virtuous activities that make up the happy life, not the external means that may seem to produce it.

– Epictetus

Life is like riding a bicycle. To keep your balance you must keep moving.

– Albert Einstein

The lessons which life, guided by infinite intelligence and invested with infinite power as it is, seeks to make available to us through the turning wheel of destiny may bring suffering but they also bring the wisdom which will shield us from suffering in the future.

-Paul Brunton

You don't get to choose how you're going to die or when. You can only decide how you are going to live.

– Joan Baaz

Life is a succession of lessons which must be lived to be understood.

– Ralph Waldo Emerson

Of all ghastly things that can happen to a man, the worst and most inexcusable is to lose interest in life.

– Herbert Casson

The Higher Life is higher living in thought, word, and deed, and knowledge of these Spiritual Principles, which are imminent in man and in the universe can only be acquired after discipline in the pursuit and practice of Value.

– James Allen

Life is still the greatest of games you can play. But you must play to win in every minute of it, with every move on the board ... Look up on all your difficulties not as stumbling blocks to trip you up, but as things waiting to be conquered.

– Paul Brunton

There is a sublime, a grand meaning behind life. It is something more than the mere round of eating, drinking and sleeping. The real life is eternal life in Atman or Spirit, a life of perfect freedom, fearlessness and bliss. It is a state of Immortality and Supreme Peace.

– Swami Sivananda

Life in this world is chaotic, fragmentary and full of unrest. The cause of suffering is the desire to enjoy the sensual objects of this world. This desire for enjoyment is due to the ignorant belief that happiness is outside you.

– Swami Sivananda

Seek to cultivate a condition where you are no longer frightened by the complexity of life, but indeed are thrilled by the challenge of trying to truly understand it.

– Andrew Cohen

A happy life must be to a great extent a quiet life, for it is only in an atmosphere of quiet that true joy can live.

– Bertrand Russell

Life is like riding a bicycle. To keep your balance you must keep moving.

– Albert Einstein

Life is larger than one's profession. Life started before we entered our professions and it is naturally assumed that it occupies only a part of our life-time. It would be wrong if it engulfs the whole of our time and consumes almost all our physical or mental energy.

– B.K. Jagdish Chander Hassija

Constructive - Positive - action of any sort brings its own immediate reward in the feeling of renewed energy, mental and physical, that follows all dynamic activity. And this uprising energy makes possible the planning of the next step in the path of advancement.

–S. Harrison

By a long habit of writing, one acquires a greatness of thinking, and a mastery of manners, which holiday writers, with ten times the genius, may vainly attempt to equal.

– Goldsmith

You have access to infinite wisdom and infinite support in every situation and under every given circumstance. But you have it only so far as you submit the ego to the higher self.

– Paul Brunton

One of the greatest adventures in living is getting to know yourself better. It is a tragedy that some individuals spend lifetime going nowhere, bogged down in frustration, because they don't know anything about themselves or how to cope with problems, many created by environment.

– Dr. Maxwell Matter

Most people live -whether physically, intellectually or morally -in a very restricted circle of their potential being. We all have reservoirs of life to draw upon of which we do not dream.

– William James

Trust yourself. Create the kind of life you will be happy to live with all your life. Make the most of yourself by fanning the tiny, inner sparks of possibility into the flames of achievement.

– Foster C. McCleslan

Live each present moment completely and the future will take care of itself. Fully enjoy the wonder and beauty of each instant. Practise the presence of peace. The more you do that, the more will feel the presence of that power in your life.

– Yogananda

Strive by every means to make your life better by ceaseless spiritual culture and practical Yoga Sadhna.

– Swami Sivananda

To live is to move with the wholeness of one's being, in harmony, to live is to move without inner friction, with the totality of one's being in harmony.

– Vimla Thakar

I really do think that any deep crisis is an opportunity to make your life extraordinary in some way.

– Martha Beck

Life is not mere living, but the enjoyment of health.

– Martial

Make it a rule of life never to regret and never to look back. Regret is an appalling waste of energy. You cannot build on it, it is only good for wallowing on.

– Katherine Mansfield

Have a purpose in life, and having it, throw into your work such strength of mind and muscle as God has given you.

– Carlyle

The important thing is not how long we live, but what we do in the time allotted to us.

– Dr. Thomas Uoolcy

LOVE

The genuine love is an expression of productiveness and implies care, respect, responsibility and knowledge. It is an active string for the growth and happiness of the loved person, rooted in one's own capacity to love.

-Eric Fromm

Unselfish love has enormous creative and therapeutic potentialities, far greater than most people think. Love is a life giving force, necessary for physical, mental, and moral health.

– Pitrim A. Sorokin

The whole world is eager to receive pure love. We should distribute it without expecting anything in return. Give it, with no desire for reciprocation.

– Swami Vivekananda

To love is to have that extraordinary feeling of affection without asking anything in return.

– J. Krishnamurti

Love is everything whether you are rich or poor; it is the emotional capital that counts most.

– Bryce Courtenay

Love is critical to a successful relationship and, when divorced from ego, is able to be given away freely and easily, resulting in a wonderful sense of fulfilment.

– Greg Vance

To build up your life upon universal love is to reap the rich harvest of real peace and happiness.

– Swami Sivananda

To love God, excluding the world, is to give Him an intense but imperfect adoration.

– Sri Aurobindo

There exists a great gift in giving unconditional love to those around you. Give nothing but love without asking for anything in return. For when you give in this manner you receive the greatest blessing and gift of all, the joy and fulfilment that infuses you with an understanding of your purpose in life.

– Greg Vance

By love I do not mean any natural tenderness, which is more or less in people according to their constitution; but I mean a larger principle of the soul, founded in reason and piety, which makes us tender, kind and gentle to all our fellow creatures as creatures of God, and for his sake.

-William Law

Love is infallible; it has no errors, for all errors are the want of love.

– William Law

Let everyone understand that real love of God does not consist in tear - shedding, nor in that sweetness and tenderness for which usually we long, just because they console us, but in serving God in justice, Fortitude of soul and humility.

– St. Teresa

A happy marriage is a new beginning of life, a new starting-point for happiness and usefulness.

– Dean Stanley

All men require something to poetize their natures, and the love of an estimable woman surely does this.

– Bayard Taylor

A great many difficulties arise from falling in love with the wrong person.

– Ruskin

Love may be, and is with a good man, the greater and better part of his life, but it is not all his life. It is unfortunately true that with a woman, love - the love she bears her husband - is her 'whole existence.'

– Orison Swett Marden

Love does not dominate, it cultivates.

– Goethe

The distinguishing marks of love, it should be evident, are disinterestedness, tranquillity and humility. When love is selfish, it can be destroying; it will destroy him who gives and him who takes. It is twice cursed. It is better not to love than to love selfishly.

– M.V. Kamath

As soon as a person can truly learn to love the disagreeable or restrictive person with whom he is involved, he will be released from this bondage.

– Gina Cerminara

Accord and harmony in family life cannot be brought about by any of the articles of comfort or luxury in the house. Accord and harmony arc the ripe fruit of mutual of love. In the absence of love the essence of family life is missing. The body is well attired. But there is no life within!

– Swami Jagadatmananda

We can get along with a little money in this world if we will; but love is a quality of which we need to possess in abundance and of which we cannot have too much.

– Orison Swett Marden

Love is the elixir of life. It has been found to have power even to cure physical and mental disorders.

– Swami Jagadatmananda

Real love is selfless and free from fear. It pours itself out upon the object of its affection without demanding any return. Its joy is in the joy of giving. Love is God in manifestation and the strongest magnetic force in the universe.

– Florence Scovel Shinn

MEDITATION

Meditation is a specific technique for resting the mind and attaining a state of consciousness that is totally different from the normal working state.

– Swami Ram

⁓⟫∘⟪⁓

Meditation has been glorified as the most scared vacation. Humans alone are capable of this highest effort by which they can hasten their own evolution.

– Swami Chinmayananda

⁓⟫∘⟪⁓

Meditation is a powerful tonic. During meditation there is generally a tremendous acceleration of energy to the individual cells... Thus the interior world takes direction from the mind and promotes physical health, mental activity, and tranquillity.

– Swami Vishnu Devananda

⁓⟫∘⟪⁓

The man who is prone to impatience, irritability, and anger needs meditation even more than other men. He needs its harmonizing effect on the whole personality, its pacifying touch on the darker impulses and passions.

– Paul Brunton

⁓⟫∘⟪⁓

Meditation on God is the most effective way of controlling the mind. Meditation and control of the mind go hand in hand. The highest objective for which one controls the mind is meditation of God or Atman as the case may be.

– Swami Budhananda

Those who start the practice of transcendent in deep meditation feel more energetic, have greater clarity of mind and better health. They become more efficient and energetic in all fields of activity.

– Mahesh Yogi

It has been scientifically proven that during meditation favourable chemicals changes take place in the brain, unlike in sleep. Meditation is a powerful weapon in the armoury of man to maintain good health and prevent diseases.

– P.C. Ganesan

Meditation is a powerful tonic. It is a mental and nerving tonic as well. The holy vibrations penetrate all the cells of the body and cure the diseases of the body. Those who meditate save doctor's bills.

– Swami Sivananda

The majority of men live in a series of conflicting desires passions, emotions and speculations, and there are restlessness, uncertainty, and sorrow, but when a man begins to train his mind in meditation, he gradually gains control over the inward conflict by bringing his thought to a focus upon a central principle.

— James Allen

The greatest help to spiritual life is meditation.

— Vivekananda

Regular meditation opens the avenues of intuitional knowledge, makes the mind calm and steady, awakens and ecstatic feeling and brings the Yogic student in contact with the source of the Supreme Purusha.

— Swami Omkarananda

Meditation is a process where the mind flows continuously towards God like an unbroken stream of oil. When 'Japa' becomes intensified it culminates in meditation.

— Swami Jagadatmananda

Through the gateway of meditation I will enter God's temple of peace everlasting. There I will worship Him at the altar of ever new contentment. I will kindle the fire of happiness to illuminate this temple within.

— Yogananda

Meditation implies awareness, awareness of the earth, the beauty of the earth, the dead leaf, the dying daylight, to be aware of the beauty of the wind among the leaves, to be aware of your thoughts, your feelings.

– J. Krishnamurti

Meditation is the art of uniting with Reality.

– Swami Krishnananda

MORAL VALUES

An honest man is the noblest work of God.

– Pope

A straight line is the shortest in morals as well as in geometry.

-Issac Barrow

The truly great are not those who have more money or brains or higher social position. God does not think less of people because they are poor or unintelligent. What matters is whether we have been kind to others and honest and sincere with ourselves and in our intimate relations with others.

– Dr. S. Radhakrishnan

Our wrong-doing produces sorrows, not only for others but principally for ourselves. Our good action produces a rebound of good fortune. We may not escape from the operation of this subtle law of moral responsibility.

– Paul Brunton

Lack of ethics is one of the main problems of polities in India today. It leads to corruption and the obvious result is inefficiency ...I would expect a combination of successful entrepreneurship and ethics to bring in accountability into the system, which we lack so badly today.

— *Narayana Murthy*

We must put out of our minds every weakening impulse by instant reference to the strength of the Over self, every evil thought by a call to the infinite good of the Over self. In this way character is uplifted and made noble.

— *Paul Brunton*

Our leaders merely put up an act before themselves and the world; they don't actually possess the values they flaunt. They use the chaos and suffering of people to step into the seat of power.

— *Mahesh Bhatt*

The worth of a life is measured by its moral value.

— *Lord Avebury*

He that would govern others first should be the master of himself.

— *Massinger*

Once to every man and nation comes the moment to decide, In the strife of Truth with Falsehood, for the good or evil side.

— *Lowell*

The unethical degradations which admittedly exist in business, political and social worlds cannot be made to disappear by running away from them but rather by the uplifting influence of individuals with superior personal character entering into them.

– Paul Brunton

PRAYER

It is' better in prayer to have a heart without words than words without a heart.

– Mahatma Gandhi

Another lesson I learned was that the intensity of prayer is not measured by time, but by the reality and depth of one's awareness of unity with God. I learned to look on prayer not as a means of influencing the creator in my favour, but as an awareness of the presence of God-everywhere.

– Margeret G, Bondfield

True prayer is more than asking; it is submission - it is union with the will and purposes of God. Prayer in this spirit gives poise and confidence to the life, and not least in moments of crisis.

– George Lyndon Carpenter

We can offer prayer standing or sitting before the image or picture of our favourite deity. It is true those who can visualize the picture of God in their heart need no external image to pray. The essential requisites of a prayer are devotion, faith and earnestness.

– Swami Jagadatmananda

True prayer is a direct raising of the mind and heart to God, without intermediary. This and nothing else is the true essence of prayer.

– Johannes Tauler

Pray for knowledge and light, every other prayer is selfish.

– Swami Vivekananda

God grant me: the serenity to accept the things I cannot change, the courage to change the things I can, and the wisdom to know the difference. Prayer should be the key of the day and the lock of the night.

– Thomas Fuller

The first rule. in prayer is to approach God only with legitimate desires. The second is to pray for their fulfilment, not as a beggar, but as a son "I am thy child. Thou art my father. Thou'and I are one."

– Paramahansa Yogananda

Prayer generates good spiritual currents and produces a rare tranquility of the mind; it elevates the whole emotional nature and is accompanied by the growth of inward grace, inner strength, and a sense of at-onement with the Supreme Being.

– Swami Omkarananda

Prayer is not to be scorned by anyone. We minify the power of the Overself if we do not accept this statement. So long as we are imperfect so long may be find it necessary to pray. So long as we find lack of anything so long may we have to pray.

– *Paul Brunton*

While you are saying your prayers, your mind is wandering every where and thinking about everything else. When you are praying, put your whole attention upon what you are saying; keep your mind on the one to whom you arc addressing your prayers.

– *Swarni Yogananda*

True prayer is not merely asking but it is much more than that. It is submission i.e., union with the will and purpose of God. Prayer in this spirit gives poise and confidence to the life, and not least in moments of crises.

– *George Lyndon Carpenter*

Prayer is the most powerful energy one can generate. As a physician, I had seen that when all therapies failed, it was sincere prayer by the patients and relations helped them in their recover.

– *Dr. Alexis Carrel*

To pretend to devotion without great humility and renunciation of all worldly tempers is to pretend to impossibilities. He that would be devout must first be humble, have a full sense of his own miseries and wants and the vanity of the world, and then his soul will be full of desire after God. A proud, or vain, or worldly-minded may use a manual of prayers, but he cannot be devout, because devotion is the application of humble heart to God as its only happiness.

– *William Law*

Man's need for prayer is as great as his need for bread. As food is necessary for the body, prayer is necessary for the soul. I have not a shadow of doubt that the strife and quarrels with which our atmosphere is so full today are due to the absence of the spirit of true prayer. True prayer never goes unanswered. When the mind is full of playful thoughts, everything in the world seems good and agreeable. Prayer is essential for progress of life.

– *Mahatma Gandhi*

Prayer should be the key of the day and lock of the night.

– *Thomas Fuller*

There are no problems that cannot be solved by prayer, no suffering that cannot be allayed by prayer, and no difficulties that cannot be surmounted by prayer, and no evil that cannot be overcome by prayer.

– *Swami Sivananda*

RELATIONSHIPS

Your marriage, friendship and business relationship can improve dramatically when you focus on sending out love rather than demanding attention, compliance, or love in return.

– Greg Vance

It makes you feel so sad that man has not discovered the secret of living. The secret is to relate oneself harmoniously on various levels in various fields of action.

– Vimla Thakar

If you would win a man to your cause, first convince him that you are his sincere friend.

– Abraham Lincoln

Relationships for us, instead of becoming occasions of joy, opportunities for sharing, events for relating one to the life around oneself, become problems that scare us.

– Vimla Thakar

One of the fundamental principles that supports our power in relationships is our willingness to create room for the other person's stuff. By stuff I mean the way they view others, the world and themselves, especially when it is different from and in opposition to our perspective.

– Dr. Joe Rubino

To be able to do the things you want to do in both your personal and professional life, you need the support and cooperation of other people-a key core belief.

– Walter Doyle Staples

In essence, superior human relations involve adding value to other people because they, like you, deserve it.

–Walter Doyle Staples

Friendships add a great deal to life, and lasting friendships arise usually between people interested in the same subject or activity. And on this ground alone, interests are of immense value in life.

– S. Harrison

In later life most people find it rather difficult to make new friends. But since the desire to give and to receive affection persists throughout life, enduring satisfaction can only be attained through happy friendships.

– S. Harrison

It has been rightly said that behind every great man there is a woman. It is not often realised that woman has willingly allowed herself to be the junior partner in a relationship in which the man grows under his wife's utter selflessness.

– M.V. Kamath

Don't cultivate friends or companions who live a low-level life and who are layabouts and wasters. Don't seek friends of inferior intellect so that you can boost your moral by talking over their heads or down to them.

– Gilbert Oaklay

Friendship is the jewel of human life and a friendless man is much to be pitied.

– Lord Avebury

If we don't let go of a resentment, anger, or hateful feeling, we are stuck with the effects of that feeling, and we begin to contaminate our own life.

– Richtird Carlson and Jossph Bailey

SPIRITUALITY

To attain spiritual realisation or to manifest the divinity within us, 'japa sadhana' is one of the best means according to all our spiritual masters.

— *Swami Gokulananda*

The great awareness comes slowly, piece by piece. The path of spiritual growth is a path of lifelong learning.

— *Anon*

To be a spiritual being ... means to employ the highest force of creativity that is possible among people.

— *Harold Klemp*

To not give credence to the spiritual life, is to deny the validity of human experience.

— *Albert Einstein*

The spiritual purpose of life is to learn to give and to receive love.

— *Harold Klemp*

By grace I mean an inner harmony, essentially spiritual, which can be translated into outward harmony.

— *Anne Morrow Lindbergh*

We are not only what we know of ourselves but an immense more which we do not know; our momentary personality is only a bubble on the ocean of our existence.

– Sri Aurovindo

Spiritualisation of life does not mean that you should abandon your family and all activities. Spiritual life gives a meaning and imparts glory to human life.

– Swami Sivananda

He who would win high spiritual degrees, must pass endless tests and examinations. But most are anxious only to bribe the examiner.

– Sri Aurobindo

Spirituality teaches us that the purpose of human existence is growth and that every situation and experience is a teacher come to home and shape us into greater perfection and wholeness.

– Suma Varughese

Spirituality is not an intellectual idea but a conviction that one is not just the body and mind, but one is part of the eternal Self, of which all other entities in the universe are also a part. This conviction may be fashioned by several factors like one's upbringing, experiences and spiritual practices.

– Pawan Kapoor

As you come to see more of the spiritual horizon of your life, you find you have a greater capacity to plan and live a happier life.

– Herold Klemp

Spirituality teaches us that there is a Higher Power running our lives and whatever comes to us, comes through that Power. Therefore what we are destined for will happen. And contrarily, what we are not destined for will not happen.

– Suma Varughese

It is spiritual culture and ethical culture alone that can change wrong racial tendencies for the better.

– Swami Vivekananda

Only a life of goodness and honesty leaves us feeling spiritually healthy and human.

– Harold Kushner

Those who have grown the most spiritually are those who are experts in living. And there is yet another joy, even greater. It is the joy of communion with God.

– M. Scott Peck

Karma is the reaction which arises from certain causes and

produces certain results. Karma is this chain of cause and effect.

– J. Krishnamurti

The most important thing is God's blessing and if you believe in God and believe in yourself, you have nothing to worry about.

– Mohamed Al-Fayed

When I admire the wonder of a sunset or the beauty of the moon, my soul expands in worship of the Creator.

– Mahatma Gandhi

God is not a mute unfeeling Being. He is love itself. If you know how to meditate to make contact with Him, He will respond to your loving demands. You do not have to plead; you can demand as His child.

– Yogananda

The surest sign of the higher life is serenity. Moral progress results in freedom from inner turmoil. You can stop fretting about this and that.

– Epictetus

Let go of all efforts, search and desires, for He can be felt only in deep peace and stillness.

– Sri Sri Ravi Shankar

For today, if you keep God by your side, there is nothing that will come into your life that you won't be able to handle.

– Vikas Malkani

There is only one way to cope with life, namely, to find that system of values which is not subject to fashionable trends ... which will never change, and will always bear good fruit in terms of bringing us peace and health and assurance, even in the midst of a very insecure world.

– Dr. Thomas Hora

The orientation of modern spirituality, under the changed conditions of today, is not towards retreat from the world but towards a spiritualizing effort in the world.

– Paul Brunton

Long identification with the material world has trained you that the false is true, that the temporary is eternal. You have to re-educate yourself into the right vision.

– Sathya Sai Baba

Man falls into a sinful state, when attainment of material desires and sense gratification become the sole pursuit of life.

– Mahatma Gandhi

One whose inner being is purified, controlled, and concentrated is able to live in the world and yet not be of the world, is able to go through worldly experiences and happenings and yet not pulled out of his or her tranquil centre by them.

– Paul Brunton

SUCCESS

The road to success is a straight and narrow path, it is a road of loving absorption, of undivided attention.

– Florence Scovel Shinn

No matter who you are or what your age may be, if you want to achieve permanent, sustaining success, the motivation that will drive you toward that goal must come from within.

– Paul J. Meyer

The quality of a person's life is in direct proportion to his commitment to excellence, regardless of his chosen field of endeavour.

– Victor Lonbaradt

Creating a successful life might be as simple as determining which moments are the most valuable, and seeing how many of those I can string together in a line.

– Pam Houston

The toughest thing about success is that you have got to keep on being a success.

– Irving Berlin

Try not to be a man of success but rather try to be a man of value.

– Albert Einstein

To win without risk is to triumph without glory.

– Corncille

There are two ways of rising in the world, either by your own industry or by the folly of others.

– La Bruyere

Excellence is doing ordinary things extraordinary well.

– Jose Ortega Y Gasset

If you want to achieve excellence, you can get there today. As of this second, quit doing less-than-excellent work.

– Thomas J. Watson

Perfection is not attainable. But if we chase perfection, we can catch excellence.

– Vince Lombardi

There are no speed limits on the road to excellence.

– David W Johnson

The individual who hopes for success must become that success in his own mind, at once. He must build his plan as perfectly as a draftsman draws the pictured house, or the sculptor sets his sketch. Nothing can ever pass into form that has not first been projected in consciousness.

– Julia Seton

Creating a successful life might be as simple as determining which moments are the most valuable, and seeing how many of those I can string together in a line.

– Pam Houston

The great and glorious master-piece of man is to know how to live to purpose.

– Montaigne

Desire is the key to motivation, but it's the determination and commitment to an unrelenting pursuit of your goal - a commitment to excellence - that will enable you to attain the success you seek.

– Merio Andretti

Stand up, be bold, be strong. Take the whole responsibility on your shoulders and know that you are the creator of your own destiny. All the strength and succour you want is within yourself. Therefore make your own future.

– Swami Vivekananda

In the final analysis there is no other solution to man's progress but the day's honest work, the day's honest activities, the day's generous utterances and the day's good deeds.

– Clare Booth Luce

Throw away all ambition beyond that of doing the day's work well. The travellers on the road to success live in the present, heedless of taking the thought of morrow. Live neither in the past nor in the future, but let each day's work absorb your entire energies and satisfy your widest ambition.

– Sir William Osler

Success is making measurable progress in reasonable time.

– Jim Rohn

Glory lies not in never falling, but in rising every time we fall.

– Nelson Mandela

Your success in life does not altogether depend on ability and training, it also depends on your determination to grasp opportunities that are presented to you. Opportunities in life come by creation, not by chance.

– Yogananda

There is no philosophy which will help a man to succeed when he is always doubting his ability to do so, and thus attracting failure. The man who would succeed, must think upward. He must think progressively, creatively, constructively, inventively, and above all, optimistically.

– Orison Swett Marden

The path to success is to take massive, determined action.

– Anthony Robbins

Success lies at the farther end of failure.

– Brian Tracy

The secret of success is constancy to purpose.

– Benjamin Disraeli

There is great power in focusing on what you want. The person who tries to do everything accomplishes nothing.

– Robin Sharma

Destiny is not a matter of chance. It is a matter of choice. It is not a thing to be waited for, it is a thing to be achieved.

– W.J. Bryan

Men hunt after petty success and trivial masteries from which they fall back into exhaustion and weakness; meanwhile all the infinite force of God in the universe waits vainly to place itself at their disposal.

– Sri Aurobindo

The men at the top climbed up because they STUDIED their jobs - kept on observing and thinking while they were at work.

– Herbert Casson

Success means doing the best we can with what we have, success is the doing, not the getting - in the trying, not the triumph.

– Wynn Davis

In truth, the only difference between those who have failed and those who have succeeded lies in the difference of their habits.

– Og Mandin

Nothing great is ever achieved without enthusiasm.

– Ralph Weldo Emerson

The person who gets the furthest is generally the one who is willing to do and dare.

– Dale Carnegie

Coming together is a beginning. Keeping together is progress. Working together is success.

– Henry Ford

All successful people have a goal. No one can get anywhere unless he knows where he wants to go and what he wants to be or do.

– Norman V. Peale

With ordinary talent and extraordinary perseverance, all things are attainable.

– Thomas Buxton

Virtually nothing on earth can stop a person with a positive attitude who has his goal clearly in sight.

– Denis Waitley

The secret of success in life is for a man to be ready for opportunity when it comes.

– Benjamin Disraeli

To me success can only be achieved through repeated failure and introspection.

– Soichiro Honda

Success is the child of audacity.

– Beaconsfield

People sometimes attribute my success to my genius. All the genius I know anything about is hard work.

– Alexander Itamilton

The most readily identifiable quality of a total winner is an overall attitude of personal optimum and enthusiasm.

– Denis Waitley

THOUGHT POWER

Any idea held in the mind that is either feared or revered will begin at once to clothe itself in the most convenient and appropriate physical form available.

– Andrew Carnegie

The ancestor of every action is a thought.

– Emerson

All achievements, whether in the business, intellectual, or spiritual world, are the result of definitely directed thought, are governed by the same law and are of the same method; the only difference lies in the object of attainment.

– James Allen

If we sow the charitable, magnanimous, encouraging uplifting thought, we shall reap the golden harvest of harmony and beauty, we shall tend to reap prosperity; while if we sow the mean, pinched, stingy failure thoughts, we shall reap a poverty harvest.

-Orison Swett Marden

Since many of our worries and fears are never likely to eventuate it is obviously our attitude of mind that is at fault. We have slipped into an unhealthy mental habit, and only "positive" activity will eradicate this.

– S. Harrison

Of all the beautiful truths pertaining to the soul which have been restored and brought to light in this age, none is more gladdening or fruitful of divine promise and confidence that this - that man is master of thought, the moulder of character, and the maker and shaper of condition, environment, and destiny.

– James Allen

We are not the victims of luck or anything else. What we are today is the result of our actions and thoughts.

– Harold Klemp

We are what our thoughts have made us; so take care of what you think.

– Swami Vivekananda

Mind is the most mysterious, the most awe-inspiring product which nature has produced, and at the same time it is the least understood, and the most often abused, of man's profound gifts from the creator.

– Napolean Hill

There is no philosophy which will help a man to succeed when he always doubts his ability to do so, and thus attracting failure. The man who would succeed must think success, must think upward. He must think progressively, creatively, constructively, inventively, and, above all, optimistically.

– Orison Swett Marden

Everyone should understand and practise auto-suggestion. Its results are marvellous. Whatever medicine can do, can be accomplished by this psychic method. You can get rid of diseases and acquire health, power, energy and vitality. This practice is an offshoot of Vedanta. It is nothing new to India. The term "auto-suggestion" is only a new colouring and garb.

– Swami Sivananda

A particular train of thought persisted in, be it good or bad, cannot fail to produce its results on the character and circumstances.

– James Allen

You are where your thoughts and actions during the past few years have brought you. Whatever you will be experiencing in your next ten or twenty years will be influenced by what you do today.

– Andrew Mathews

Human beings possess capabilities of mind that are literally beyond genius.

– Barbara Brown

Despite the vast amount being discovered about the brain's fantastic capacity and the ways in which it works, few people know how to make the best use of their brains.

– Peter Russel

The highest possible stage in moral culture is when we recognize that we ought to control our thoughts.

– Charles Darwin

Change your thoughts and you change your world.

– Norman Vincent Peale

When your inner dialogue constantly stresses scarcity, unworthiness or ugliness, how can you create the life you want? You can't-keep saying or writing affirmations until the negative retorts cease.

– Joyce Strum

An open mind is the beginning of self-discovery and growth. We can't learn anything new until we can admit that we don't already know everything.

– Erwin G. Hall

Man after becomes what he believes himself to be. If I keep on saying to myself that I cannot do a certain thing, it is possible that I may end by really becoming incapable of doing it. On the contrary, if I have the belief that I can do it, I shall surely acquire the capacity to do it even if I may not have it at the beginning.

– M.K. Gandhi

Don't limit yourself. Many people limit themselves to what they think they can do. You can go as far as your mind lets you. What you believe, you can achieve.

– Mary Kay Ash

Mind is the chief factor governing the body. One should always avoid suggesting to the mind thoughts of human limitations: sickness, old age, and death.

– Yogananda

The same strength which is put into negative thoughts like fear, grief, revenge, and discord-to your own detriment-can be put into positive ones like courage, cheerfulness, fortitude, benevolence, and calmness, to your own benefit.

– Paul Rrunton

The greatest discovery of my generation is that human beings can alter their lives by altering their attitudes of mind.

– William James

Since many of our worries and fears are never likely to eventuate it is obviously our attitude of our mind that is at fault. We have slipped into an unhealthy mental habit, and only "positive" activity will eradicate this.

– *S. Harrison*

That which we experience inwardly as thought must, if it be strong and sustained enough, manifest, itself outwardly in events or environment or both.

– *Paul Brunton*

Right thinking and right living make a right life. The body, being the product of the mind, must necessarily be like it.

– *Orison Swett Marden*

Thoughts unexpressed can also go out as forces and produce their effects. It is a mistake to think that a thought or will can have effect only when it is expressed in speech or act: the unspoken thought, the unexpressed will are also active energies and can produce their own vibrations, effects or reactions.

– *Sri Aurobindo*

TIME

Time and space are infinite, and therefore have neither beginning nor end.

-Swami Vivekananda

․

If you love life, don't waste time, for time is what life is made up of.

– Bruce Lee

․

There is no such thing as lack of time. We all have plenty of time to do everything we really want to do.

– Alan Lakein

․

We always have time enough, if we will but use it right.

– Goethe

․

We never shall have more time. We have, and we have always had, all the time there is.

– Arnold Bennett

․

Every morning when the alarm goes off, we have a totally new opportunity to do what we want with the hours we have been gifted. And we are gifted with that clean slate every day for the rest of our lives.

– Hyrum Smith

Always concentrate on the most valuable use of your time. This is what separates the winners from the losers.

– Brian Tracy

Time is life. It is irreversible and irreplaceable. To waste your time is to waste your life, but to master your time is to master your life and make the most of it.

– Alan Lakein

Men talk of killing time, while time quietly kills them.

– Dion Boucicault

There is a simple test by which you may judge whether or not you have been using your Time to best advantage. If you have attained peace of mind and material opulence sufficient for your needs, your Time has been properly used. If you have not attained these blessings, your Time has not been properly used, and you should begin now to search for the circumstances in connection with which you have fallen short.

– Nepolean Hill

MISCELLANEOUS

There is always something abnormal and eccentric about men of genius. And why not? For genius itself is an abnormal birth and out of man's ordinary centre.

– Sri Aurobindo

A religion that takes no account of practical affairs, and does not help in them, is no religion.

– Mahatma Gandhi

Nothing gives one person so much advantage over other as to remain cool and unruffled under all circumstances.

– Thomas Jefferson

The root cause of stress is the ego and the sense of identification with the body.

– Dada J.P. Vaswani

'Maya' arising from a combination of lust and desire is the force that drives a man to self gratification -it bends the soul to the material world.

– Mahatma Gandhi

The first test of a truly great man is his humility.

– John Ruskin

There are many paths to the centre, but the signposts are all the same - passion, peace, love, and a reverence for life.

– Jennifer James

Suffering could build strength, but only if a person acknowledges his or her responsibility for whatever went wrong.

– Elerold Klemp

Knowledge is a child with its achievements, for it has found out something, it runs about the streets whooping and shouting; Wisdom conceals hers for a long time in a thoughtful and mighty silence.

– Sri Aurobindo

We have to penetrate the cluttered noisiness of our mind and the world around us to reach where absolute silence alone remains. When we know silence, we shall know ourselves.

– Anuradha Vashisht

If life alone were and not death, there could be no immortality; if love were alone and not cruelty, joy would be only a tepid and ephemeral rapture, if reason were alone and not ignorance, our highest attainment would not exceed a limited rationality and worldly wisdom.

– Sri Aurobindo

Before we can help others or influence the world, we need to possess three things: knowledge, experience, and power.

– Paul Brunton

There are many things we do not like as we go through life, but if these are unalterable we must learn to adapt ourselves to existing conditions. It is no use fretting over what cannot be altered; we have to accept things as they are. Only by doing this shall we ever have a contented mind.

– S. Harrison

Any time you have difficulty making an important decision, you can be sure that it's the result of being unclear about your values.

– Anthony Robbins

The richness of human experiences would lose something of rewarding joy if there were no limitations to overcome.

– Helen Keller

We are not rich by what we possess but rather by what we can do without.

– Immanuel Kant

When you are sorrowful, look again in your heart, and you shall see that in truth you are weeping for that which has been your delight.

– Kahlil Gibran

All our dreams can come true - if we have the courage to pursue them.

– Walt Disney

The reasonable man adapts himself to the conditions that surround him. The unreasonable man adapts surrounding conditions to himself. All progress depends on the unreasonable man.

– George Bernard Shaw

Great minds have purposes, others have wishes.

– Washington Irving

Become a possibilitarian. No matter how dark things seem to be or actually are, raise your rights and see possibilities - always see them for they are always there.

– Norman Vincent Peal

Grow old gracefully. You have had your days of batting, now go and sit in the pavilion as interested spectators. Let the young people play their games without much interference. Encourage them. Give advice only when they seek or welcome it.

– Yogi Raushan Nath

Blessed is he who has found his work; let him ask no other blessedness. He has a work, a life purpose; he has found it, and will follow it.

– Carlyle

Mother Earth is having sufficient for man's need but not for his greed.

– Mahatma Gandhi

Real glory springs from the conquest of ourselves, and without that, the conqueror is naught but the veriest slave.

– Thomson

Pleasant words are as a honeycomb, sweet to the soul and health to the bones.

– Solomon

Strength of character consists of two things, power of will and power of self-restraint. It requires two things, therefore, for its Existence, strong feelings and strong command over them.

– F.W. Robertson

Vacillation is the prominent feature of weakness of character.

– Voltaire

◦◦◦

Hypocrisy desires to seem good rather than to be so; honesty desires to be good rather than to seem so.

– Warwick

◦◦◦

Any time you have difficulty making an important decision, you call be sure that it's the result of being unclear about your values.

– Allthony Robbins

◦◦◦

It is not hard to make decisions when you know what your values are.

– Roy Disney

◦◦◦

Reflect upon your blessings of which every man has many, not on your past misfortunes of which all men have some.

– Charles Dickens

◦◦◦

Introspection is a very healthy practice as long as you do not employ it to dwell it on your weaknesses until you are plunged into depression, or into such feelings of guilt that you begin to hate yourself. This is a misuse and abuse of self - analysis.

– Sri Sri Daya Mata

◦◦◦

Kind words can be short and easy to speak but their echoes are truly endless.

– Mother Teresa

Remember thy creator in the days of thy youth. To die as we should wish, we should live as we ought. To the good man death has no terror.

– Lord Avebury

You cannot, in any given case, by any sudden and single effort, will to be true, if the habit of your life has been insincerity.

– F.W. Robertson

If courage is gone, then all is gone.

– Goethe

Habit and Change are the two opposite qualities of Human Nature. The one leads to fixation, and the other leads to explosion, if you fail to balance the one with the other.

– Herbert Casson

Of all the gifts bestowed by nature on human beings, hearty laughter must be close to the top.

– Norman Cousins

It is our feelings about things that torment us rather than the things themselves, it follows that blaming others is silly. Therefore, when we suffer setbacks, disturbances, or grief, let us never place the blame on others, but on our own attitudes.

– Epictetus

Resolve to be tender with the young, compassionate with the aged, sympathetic with the striving and tolerant of the weak and wrong. Because some time in our lives we would have been all of these ourselves.

– Lloyd Shearer

Our privileges can be no greater than our obligations. The protection of our rights can endure no longer than the performance of our responsibilities.

– John F. Kennedy

Don't talk about yourself; it will be done when you leave.

– Wilson Mizner

Freedom is not worth having if it does not include the freedom to make mistakes.

– Mahatma Gandhi

The truly great are not those who have more money or brains or higher social position. God does not think less of people because they are poor or unintelligent. What matters is whether we have been kind to others and honest and sincere with ourselves and in our intimate relations with others.

– *S. Radhakrishnan*

A leader is a person you will follow to a place you wouldn't go by yourself.

– *Joel Barker*

There is only one corner of the Universe you can be certain of improving and that's your own self.

– *Aldous Leonard Huxley*

There is a certain degree of satisfaction in having the courage to admit one's errors. It often helps solve the problem created by the error.

– *Dale Carnegie*

Science is organized knowledge. Wisdom is organised life.

– *Immaneul Icant*

If you possess an ability that others do not, do not let it go to your head. Remember that it was God who chose to give you that ability over others.

– *Vikas Malkani*

Perceiving the world as 'Me and mine' gives rise to attachments, You and yours' to jealously. Both deserve to be shunned.

– Mahatma Gandhi

I love those who criticize me - as they are my teachers in my path of self-growth.

– Swami Vivekananda

The most beautiful experience is the mysterious. It is this fundamental emotion which stands at the cradle of true art and true science.

– Albert Einstein

Often people think opportunity is a matter of luck. I believe opportunities are all around us. Some seize them; others stand and let them pass by.

– Dhirubhai Ambani

Money, you are the cause of the anxieties of life, and through you we go down to the grave before our time.

– Plautus

Those who think they have no time for bodily exercise will sooner or later have to find time for illness.

– Edward Stanley

Problems are not stop signs, they are guidelines.

– Robert Schuller

❦

Never depend on the admiration of others. There is no strength in it. Personal merit cannot be derived from an external source.

– Epictetus

❦

By a long habit of writing, one acquires a greatness of thinking, and a mastery of manners, which holiday writers, with ten times the genius, may vainly attempt to equal.

– Goldsmith

❦

You have access to infinite wisdom and infinite support in every situation and under every given circumstance. But you have it only so far as you submit the ego to the higher self.

– Paul Brunton

❦

One of the greatest adventures in living is getting to know yourself better. It is a tragedy that some individuals spend lifetime going nowhere, bogged down in frustration, because they don't know anything about themselves or how to copy with problems, many created by environment.

– Dr. Mascwell Maltz

❦

It is unwise to be too sure of one's wisdom. It is healthy to be reminded that the strongest might weaken and the wisest might err.

– *Mahatma Gandhi*

Confidence, like art, never comes from giving all the answers; it comes from being open to all the questions.

– *Earl Gray Stevens*

People ask you for criticism, but they only want praise.

– *W. Somerset Maugham*

Politeness and consideration for others is like inventing pennies and getting dollars back.

– *Thomas Sowell*

You can't undo the past... but you can certainly not repeat it.

– *Bruce Willis*

Have the courage of your opinions. You must expect to be laughed at sometimes and it will do you no harm. There is nothing ridiculous in seeming to be what you really are, but a good deal in affecting to be what you are not.

– *Lord Avebury*

Experience is a name everyone gives to his mistakes.

– *Oscar Wilde*

Do not expect too much and do not expect it too quickly. Everything comes to those who know how to wait.

– Lord Avebury

Habit, if wisely and skilfully formed, becomes a second nature.

– Bacon

The chain of habit coils itself around the heart like a serpent, to gnaw and stifle it.

– Hazlitt

All philosophy lies in two words "sustain" and "abstain".

– Epictetus

Perpetual pushing and assurance put a difficulty out of countenance, and make a seeming impossibility give way.

– Jeremy Collier

He who seeks only applause from without, has all his happiness in another's keeping.

– Oliver Goldsmith

It is easy to dodge our responsibilities, but we cannot dodge the consequences of dodging our responsibilities.

– Lord Stamp